THE MISSING CHICKY COMES HOME

THE MISSING CHICKY

COMES HOME

THE MISSING CHICKY
COMES HOME

A day in the farm

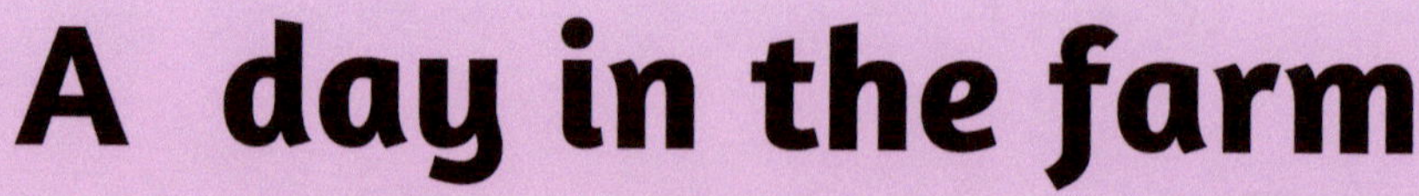

A sunny bright morning in the
house of little Chicky

The Little Chicky

My beak is getting stronger.
I think I can make some catches
myself

Little Chicky alone in thought

The family house of Chicky

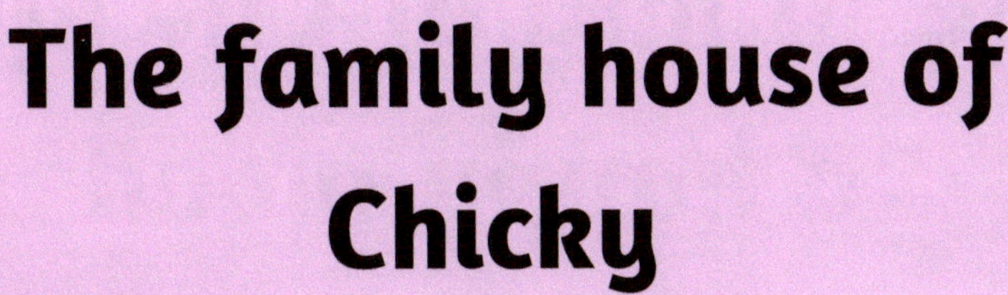

The warmth and protection of being in the fold

The family of Chicky in a happy mood

Chicky tries to sneak out from the back of Mama Chicky

Chicky sneaks out

Chicky delayed her steps facing another way

Chicky out of mama sight

Chicky stays behind

Wow a worm

I made a catch, it is a worm

Chicky filled

My beak got me a worm today. I am happy for the catch. I will catch again tomorrow.

Chicky in a happy mood after the catch

I will tell my stories to my brothers and sisters and also mama

Chicky sings

I have a beak getting stronger
I have a beak getting sharper
I love to catch and catch and catch
I have a beak getting strong

Chicky adventure continues

My wings, my wings, my wings
oh my wings in joy I swing to fly
and
My legs the earth to scratch for more
worms to catch

Chicky is missing

Mama Chicky is out to look for Chicky

Mama Chicky Clucks in search for Chicky

bwok, bwok bwok, Chicky where are you?

bwok, bwok bwok, Chicky come back home

Mama chicky tells other chicks of his missing

Chicky left the house and may be in danger now

Chicky meets a friend

I am Chicky, I lost my way home, mama will be looking for me.

Squirrel helps Chicky

Chicky is told of hawk

Hawk? Oh I am lost

Chicky get ready for home

Oh my little wings cannot fly please save me.

Chicky goes home

Oh my home , oh my home ,
when shall I see my home
when shall I see my mama
home
I will never forget my home

Chicky is home

Chicky is home safe

Chicky is home

Mama, my friend saved me
from hawks